anythink

Halloween Crafts

by Anita Yasuda • illustrated by Mernie Gallagher-Cole

The Child's World®
childsworld.com

Published by The Child's World®
1980 Lookout Drive • Mankato, MN 56003-1705
800-599-READ • www.childsworld.com

Acknowledgments
The Child's World®: Mary Swensen, Publishing Director
Red Line Editorial: Editorial direction and production
The Design Lab: Design

Photographs ©: 5 Second Studio/Shutterstock Images, 4

ISBN 9781503808201
LCCN 2015958199

Printed in the United States of America
Mankato, MN
June, 2016
PA02298

About the Author
Anita Yasuda is the author of more than 100 books for children. She enjoys writing biographies, books about science, social studies, and chapter books. Yasuda lives with her family in Huntington Beach, California, where you can find her on most days walking her dog along the shore.

About the Illustrator
Mernie Gallagher-Cole is an artist living in West Chester, Pennsylvania. She has illustrated many books, games, and puzzles for children. She loves crafts and tries to be creative every day.

Table of Contents

Introduction to Halloween

Trick or treat! It is Halloween night! On October 31 each year, children around the world dress up in costumes. Then they collect candy and treats from neighbors or friends. They might go to parties or play games. Halloween is a fun holiday.

Halloween began more than 2,000 years ago with the **festival** of Samhain. This marked the end of fall. People in Ireland and Scotland

Halloween is a fun time to wear a costume and collect candy and other treats.

celebrated the festival on November 1. It honored the dead. People believed the dead came to visit. Evil spirits also came back. The Irish and Scottish built big fires to keep the evil spirits away.

In the 600s, the **Celts** became Christian. Their festival for the dead became part of All Hallows Day. It was a day set aside by the church. Later it became known as All Hallows Eve or Halloween. **Immigrants** from Ireland and Scotland brought this holiday to the United States. They also brought with them many of its **customs**. One was telling ghost stories. Another was bobbing for apples. It was a game used to tell a person's future.

Halloween is still an exciting holiday that some people celebrate. People carve pumpkins. These pumpkins are called jack-o'-lanterns. Children make or buy their costumes. They spend weeks thinking about what they should be. On Halloween night, some children go trick-or-treating. They show their goody bags and ask for treats.

Spooky Treat Bag

Long ago, on All Hallows Eve, people went door to door. They sang songs. They offered to pray for the dead. In return, people gave them a small round cake. It was called a Soul Cake. Now many people hand out candy. This bag will hold your treats!

MATERIALS

- ☐ Pencil
- ☐ Black paper
- ☐ Scissors
- ☐ Glue
- ☐ Paper lunch bag
- ☐ Orange paper
- ☐ Green paper
- ☐ Masking tape

STEPS

1. Using the pencil, draw eyes and a mouth on the black paper. Then cut the pieces out with a scissors.

2. Glue the eyes and the mouth to the paper lunch bag. Let them dry.

3. Next, take the orange paper. Using the pencil, draw a leaf shape. Cut it out with the scissors. Use this leaf to trace several more leaves on the orange paper. Cut all the leaves out.

4. Arrange the leaves in a circle. Glue the leaves together in the center.

5. Make a vine for the bag. With the pencil, draw vertical lines on the green paper.

6. Roll the green paper widthwise. Glue it closed. The lines should be facing out.

7. Add the pumpkin topper to the bag using masking tape. Your bag is ready for treats!

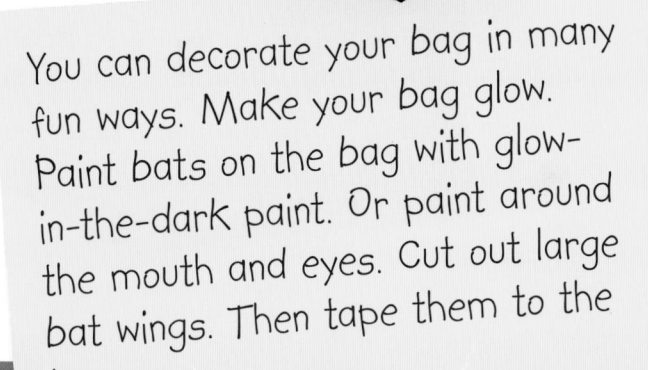

You can decorate your bag in many fun ways. Make your bag glow. Paint bats on the bag with glow-in-the-dark paint. Or paint around the mouth and eyes. Cut out large bat wings. Then tape them to the bag.

Ghostly Mask

People once thought the dead came back on Halloween. They were scared to leave their homes. They thought some spirits might be evil. Adults often hid behind masks on Halloween. By the 1800s, people dressed up for fun at parties. Children soon joined in the fun.

MATERIALS

- ☐ Pencil
- ☐ White paper
- ☐ Scissors
- ☐ Clear tape
- ☐ Paintbrush
- ☐ Silver glitter glue
- ☐ Silver glitter stars
- ☐ Black paper
- ☐ Glue
- ☐ Hole punch
- ☐ Elastic string
- ☐ Ruler

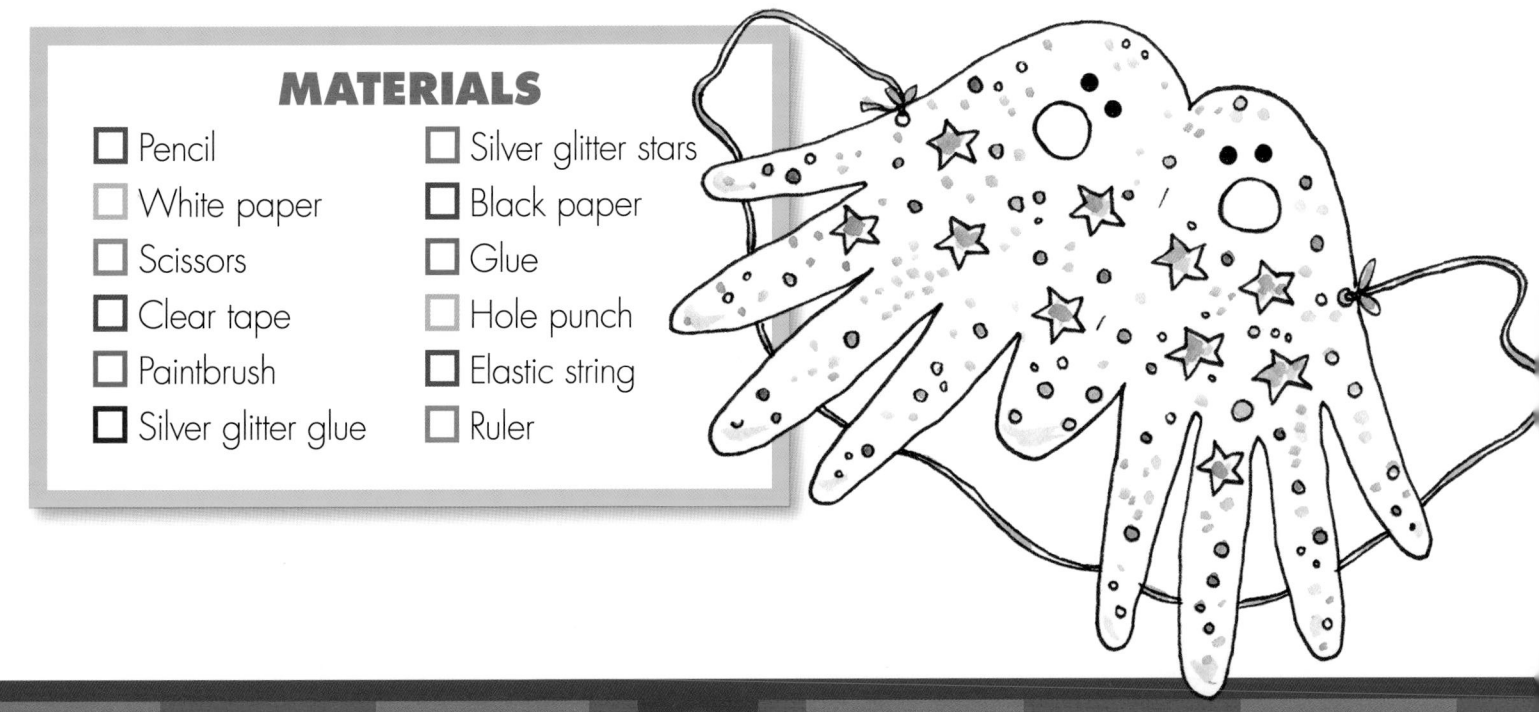

STEPS

1. Using a pencil, trace one hand at a time on the white paper. Cut the hands out with a scissors. Turn the hands upside down. The palms are the ghosts' heads. The fingers are the bottoms of the ghosts.

2. Tape the hands together at the thumbs. If the mask is too wide for your face, overlap the thumbs.

3. Next, create mouths for your ghosts. Cut a hole in the center of each hand. The hole is also your eyehole.

4. With a paintbrush, paint silver glitter glue over the ghosts. Then, sprinkle glitter stars over the glue. Let the mask dry.

5. Give your ghosts eyes. Cut four circles out of the black paper. Glue two to the top of each handprint.

6. Use the hole punch to make a small hole on the side of each hand. Cut a length of elastic string about 12 inches (30 cm) long. Tie the string to the holes. Now you can try on your mask.

You do not have to make a ghost mask. Try making a mummy mask. Trace your hands on black paper. Turn the fingers facing up. Glue strips of cotton around each finger. Glue googly eyes to each finger. Decorate the mask with glow-in-the-dark paint.

Monster Bracelet

The Celts believed in ghosts. They told stories about meeting them. People still tell scary tales at Halloween. One of the best-known stories is by Mary Shelley. The monster is called Frankenstein. What will you call your monster?

MATERIALS

- ☑ Ruler
- ☐ Green craft foam
- ☑ Scissors
- ☑ Pencil
- ☑ White paper
- ☐ Black paper
- ☐ Glue
- ☑ Aluminum foil
- ☐ Clear tape
- ☐ Pipe cleaner

STEPS

1. Measure with a ruler a rectangle 1.5 inches (3.8 cm) by 3.5 inches (8.9 cm) on the green foam. Then cut it out with scissors. This will be the monster's head.

2. With a pencil, draw spirals for the eyes on the white paper. Then draw a monster's mouth on the black paper. Cut these pieces out. Glue them to the head. Let the pieces dry.

3. Next make a bolt for the head. Cut a 2.5-inch (6.4 cm) long bolt shape from the aluminum foil. Tape it to the foam.

4. Place the monster face down. Lay the pipe cleaner across the middle. Tape it in place.

5. Bring the ends of the pipe cleaner up. Wrap the pipe cleaner loosely around your wrist.

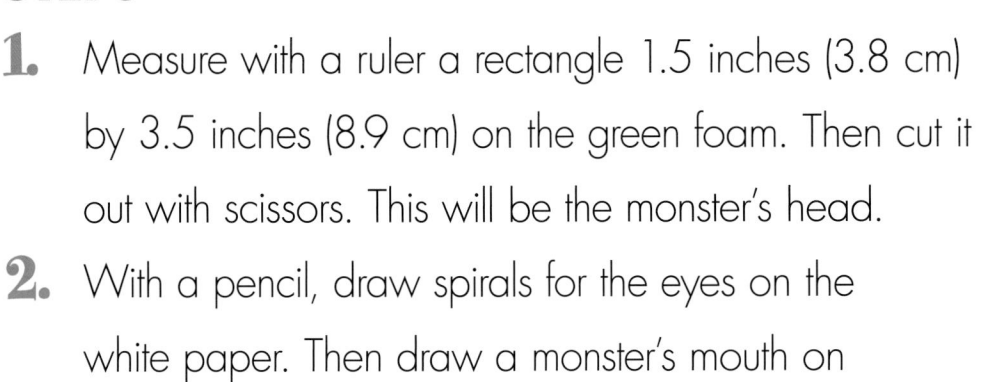

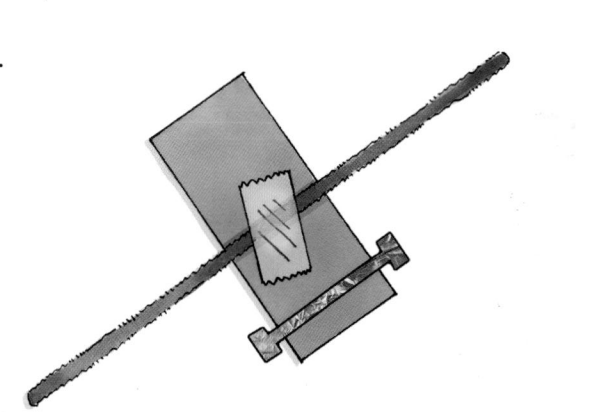

Candy Corn Cuties

Candy corn was first made in the 1880s. It became a popular Halloween treat. It reminded people of the fall. Corn is **harvested** during this season. You cannot eat this candy corn. But you can decorate your home with it.

MATERIALS

- ☐ Plastic cup
- ☐ Nine-inch paper plate
- ☐ Paintbrush
- ☐ Yellow and orange paint
- ☐ Scissors
- ☐ Black paper
- ☐ Glue stick
- ☐ Craft magnets

STEPS

1. Put a plastic cup in the middle of a paper plate. Paint two rings around the cup with a paintbrush. The inside ring will be yellow. The outside ring will be orange. The center will stay white. Let the paint dry.

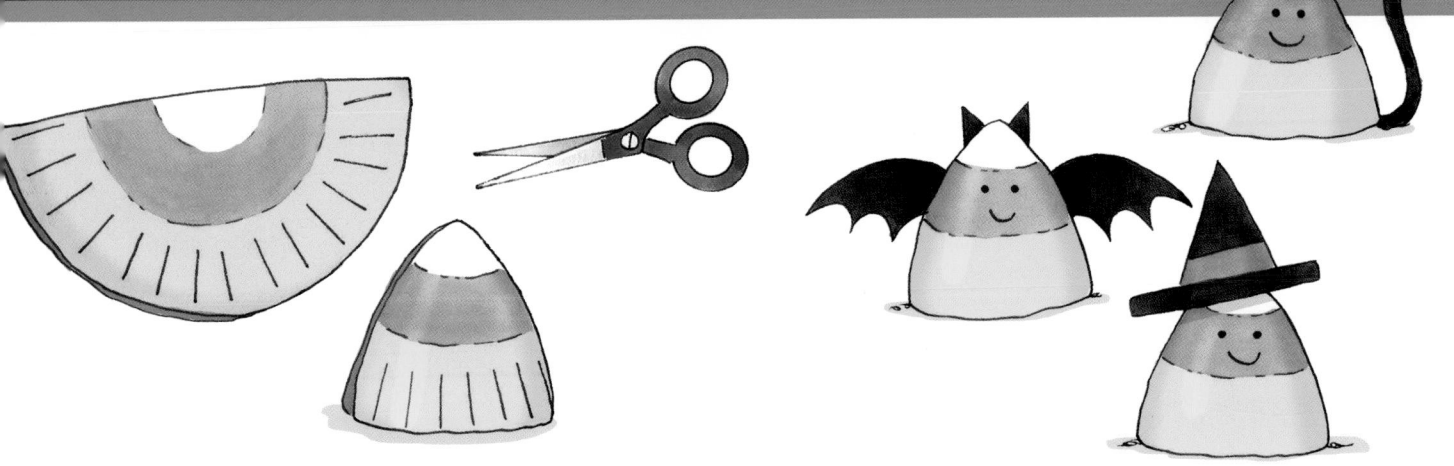

2. Fold the plate in half. Then fold it in half again. Unfold the plate and cut along the fold lines with scissors. You will have four large triangles. These are your candy corn.

3. Cut out ears, hats, or tails from the black paper. Glue them to the triangles to make cats, bats, or witches.

4. Peel off the backing from the magnets. Press them on the back of the triangles. Now decorate your refrigerator with these candy cuties!

You can do many things with the candy corns. Make a mini wreath. Cut out a circle from an empty cereal box. Then, cut out an inner circle. Wrap the wreath with black and orange ribbon. Glue the candy corn pieces on top. Tie a string to the top of the wreath and hang it up.

Wicked Web

The spider is a popular symbol of Halloween. Some people are scared of them. For others, spiders are signs of bad luck. Long ago, people did not want to see a spider on Halloween. It was said to be a spirit. Who will your spider scare?

MATERIALS

- ☐ Paper plate
- ☐ Scissors
- ☐ Pencil
- ☐ Hole punch
- ☐ Silver paint
- ☐ Paintbrush
- ☐ Black yarn
- ☐ Masking tape
- ☐ Five black pipe cleaners
- ☐ One large cotton ball
- ☐ Eight orange beads
- ☐ Glue
- ☐ Two googly eyes

STEPS

1. Cut out the center of a paper plate with scissors. You will be left with a 1.5-inch (4 cm) rim. Lightly mark 12 lines around the plate with a pencil. Evenly space them out. They will be guides for the spiderweb's holes.

2. Using a hole punch, punch a hole at each line around the inside of the circle.

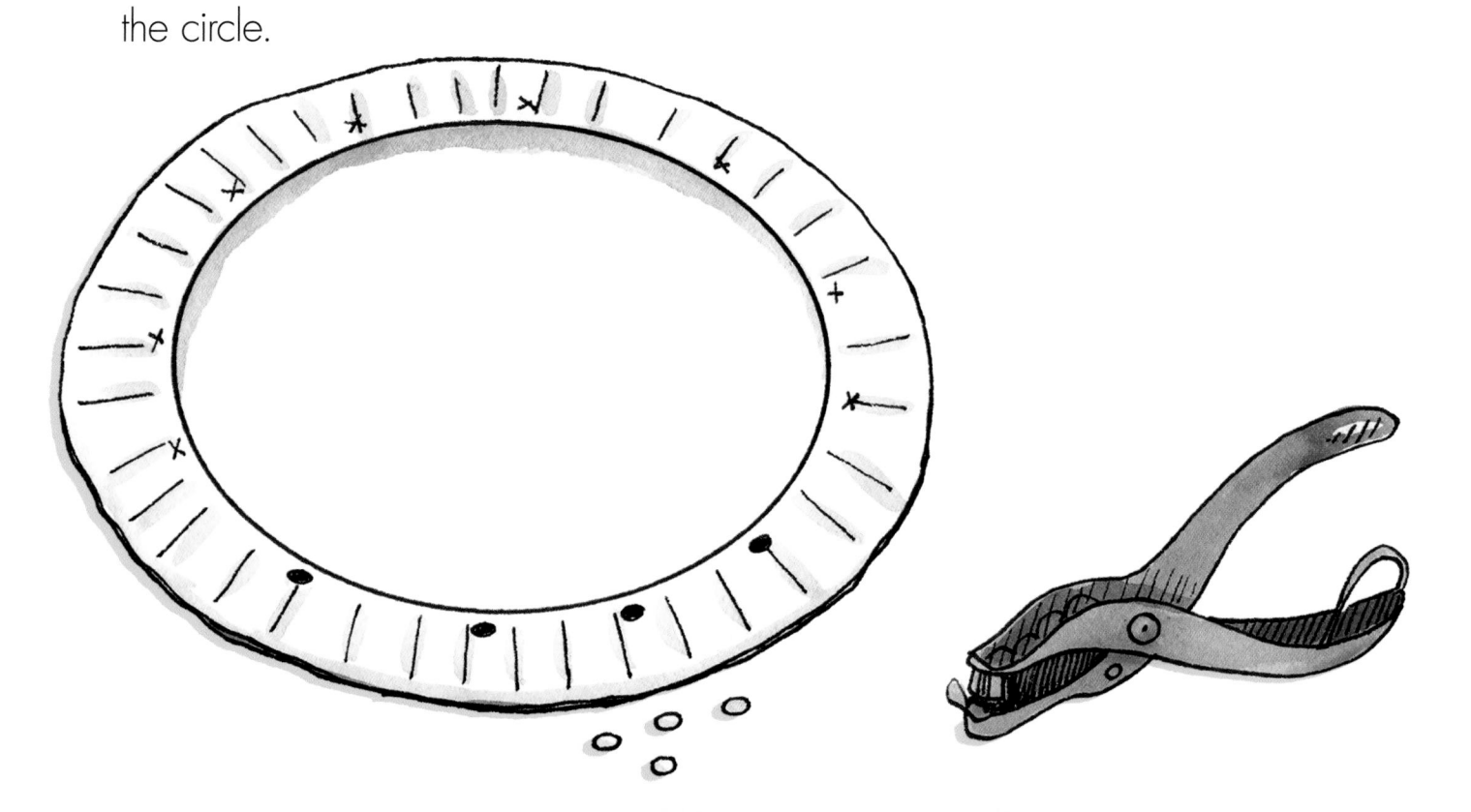

3. Paint the paper plate silver using a paintbrush. Let it dry.

4. Cut an arm's length of black yarn. Knot one end of the yarn. Wrap a piece of tape around the other end.

5. Thread the black yarn through a bottom hole. Then thread the yarn across the plate to the other side. Go in and out of all the holes, making sure to go across the plate each time. Tie a knot when you are done. Set the web to the side.

6. For the spider, wrap a black pipe cleaner around a cotton ball.

7. The spider will have four legs on each side. Cut four pipe cleaners in half. Push each leg into the body. Fan the legs out. Add an orange bead to each leg. Bend the ends downwards.

8. Glue eyes to the front of the body.

9. Tie the spider to the web with yarn. When you are done, hang your web.

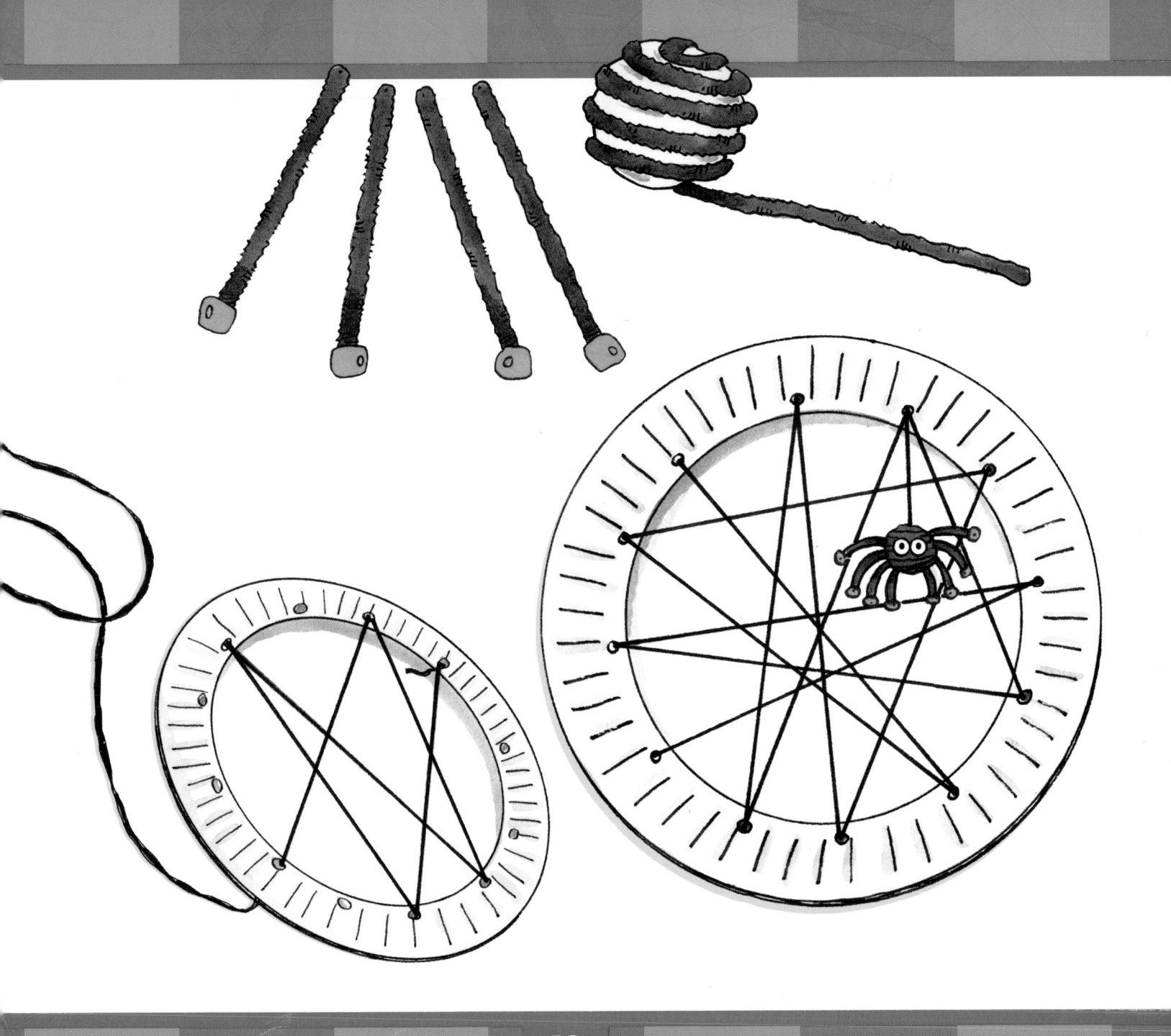

Hungry Goblin Game

People believed that scary things came out on All Hallows Eve. One creature was the goblin. It liked to play tricks on people. Make a goblin for your home. But do not forget to feed it!

MATERIALS

- [ ] Long rectangular box, such as a cracker box
- [ ] Scissors
- [ ] Red and blue paint
- [ ] Paintbrush
- [ ] Colored paper
- [ ] Glue
- [ ] Pencil
- [ ] Thread
- [ ] Button

STEPS

1. Stand your box upright. Cut the top off with a scissors.
2. Paint the entire box red with a paintbrush. Let it dry.
3. Dip the end of the paintbrush into the blue paint. Add polka dots to your box. Let it dry.

4. Cut out a mouth full of sharp teeth from the colored paper. Then glue it around the top of the box.

5. Cut a long strip of paper for the tongue. Roll the paper around a pencil to curl it. Glue it to the mouth.

6. Make two big eyes from the paper scraps. Glue them to the top edge of the box.

7. Using the scissors, poke a hole on one side near the top. Push the thread through the hole. Make a knot inside the box. Tie the other end to a button. Try to flip the button into the top of the hungry monster. *Hint*: The shorter the thread, the easier the game.

Use different colored paint to make more monster boxes. Cut out two egg carton shells. They can be used for eyes. Or play a different game. Tape four or more boxes together. Stand a few feet away. Try to toss a piece of candy into one of the boxes.

Glossary

Celts (KELTS) Celts are people who lived in Western Europe. Early Celts had a festival for the dead.

customs (KUHSS-tuhms) Customs are traditional ways of behaving. Customs were brought to the United States.

festival (FESS-tuh-vuhl) A festival is a special time or event when people gather to celebrate something. Halloween began at the festival of Samhain.

harvested (HAR-vist-ed) Harvested means crops are gathered for use. Corn is harvested in the fall.

immigrants (IM-uh-gruhnts) Immigrants are people who move to a new country to live there. Immigrants from Ireland and Scotland brought Halloween to the United States.

To Learn More

IN THE LIBRARY

Rau, Dana Meachen. *Creating Halloween Crafts.*
Ann Arbor, MI: Cherry Lake Publishing, 2014.

Sanderson, Jennifer, and Jessica Moon. *Holiday
Papercraft.* Mankato, MN: Arcturus, 2015.

Smith, Mary-Lou. *Celebrate Halloween.* New
York: Cavendish Square, 2016.

ON THE WEB

Visit our Web site for links about Halloween Crafts:
childsworld.com/links

Index